～～～Strong and Simple
Messages for Children's Ministry

by Ruth Reazin Ministry

Group
Loveland, Colorado

The most important thing we can give our children is the knowledge and assurance of God's love. It is my hope and prayer that these object lessons will help you give your children a little better understanding of this love in some small way.

—Ruth Reazin

STRONG AND SIMPLE MESSAGES FOR CHILDREN'S MINISTRY
Copyright © 1998 Ruth Reazin

Credits
Editors: Jody Brolsma and Jan Kershner
Senior Editor: Ivy Beckwith
Chief Creative Officer: Joani Schultz
Copy Editor: Julie Meiklejohn
Art Director: Jean Bruns
Cover Art Director: Jeff A. Storm
Cover Designer: Joe Ragont Design
Computer Graphic Artist: Eris Klein
Cover Illustrator: Patrick Browne
Production Manager: Peggy Naylor

Unless otherwise noted, Scriptures taken from the HOLY BIBLE, NEW INTERNA-TIONAL VERSION®. Copyright 1973, 1978, 1984 by International Bible Society. Used by permission of Zondervan Publishing House. All rights reserved.

Library of Congress Cataloging-in-Publication Data
Reazin, Ruth, 1946-
    Strong and simple messages for children's ministry / by Ruth Reazin.
        p.   cm.
    Includes indexes.
    ISBN 0-7644-2051-8
    1. Children's sermons. 2. Object-teaching. I. Group Publishing.
II. Title.
BV4315.R356   1998
268'.432--dc21   98-14421
                                                                     CIP

10 9 8 7 6 5   07 06 05 04 03 02 01
Printed in the United States of America.

Visit our web site: www.grouppublishing.com

Contents

Lessons for Any Occasion

Fire Prevention (Proverbs 15:1; James 3:5) 6

The Tools of the Trade (2 Timothy 3:16) .8

A Clear Connection (1 Timothy 2:5) 10

Only One Way (John 14:6) 12

Believin' Balloon-Blowers (Hebrews 11:1) 13

Shiny and Clean (Acts 3:19a) 14

God's Point of View (Proverbs 3:5-6) 15

The Write Stuff (1 Corinthians 12:27) .17

Lending Us a Hand (Philippians 2:13) .18

Puzzle Presents (1 Corinthians 12:4-5) 19

Vegetable Variety (Romans 12:5-6a) 20

No Call-Waiting (Zechariah 13:9b) 21

Heavy Hearts (Matthew 11:28) 22

Rise Above It (Hebrews 13:5b) 23

Important Instructions (Psalm 119:105) 24

Lessons in Life (John 16:33b) 25

The Most Wonderful Gift (Ephesians 2:8-9) 27

Cracked Jars (Exodus 4:1) 28

This Little Light (Matthew 5:15) 29

Kindness Trees (Week One) (Matthew 25:34-40;

    Ephesians 4:32) 30

Kindness Trees (Week Two) (Ephesians 4:32) 31

The Recipe for Life (Isaiah 55:9) 32

The Real Thing (1 John 4:1-2) 34

Flex Your Faith (James 2:17) 36

I Just Can't Wait (2 Peter 3:13) 37

Only a Shell (Luke 23:43) 38

Inside Out Love (1 Samuel 16:7b; James 2:1-5) 40

Two Sides of Love (Psalm 127:3b; Proverbs 13:24) 41

Where a Flower Gets Its Power (John 15:5) 43

Cool Your Heels (Psalm 27:14) 45

Ring Around My Heart (Romans 8:38-39; 1 John 4:8b) 47

Who's in Control? (James 3:3-6) 49

The "i" in Hurricane (Ephesians 4:26) 51

A Tale of Two Houses (Matthew 7:24-28) 52

A Wonderful Way to Spell "Joy" (Nehemiah 8:10b) 54

Amazing Grace (Ephesians 2:8) 56

One-Way Ticket (John 14:2; Acts 16:31a) 58

The Power Inside (Psalm 29:11a) 59

Squeaky-Clean (Psalm 51:10a; Jeremiah 2:22; 1 John 1:7) 60

The Doubtful Dough (Romans 9:20-21) 61

Big-Bang Bust (Genesis 1:1) 62

A Picture of Love (Luke 10:27b, 30-37) 64

Lessons for Special Occasions

Never Leave Home Without It (John 13:35) 66

Memories (Matthew 26:26-29) 67

With a Grateful Heart (Luke 17:11-19) 68

Rockin' Roll (Matthew 27:57-61; 28:1-7) 69

Baby Shower (Luke 2:1-16) 70

Victory in Jesus (John 12:12-13) 72

Two Precious Gifts (Romans 6:23b) 73

Daddy's Heart (1 John 3:1a) 74

Happy Birthday! (1 John 3:1a) 75

Saint Patrick (John 10:30; 14:16-17a) 76

The Head of the Class (Psalm 111:10a) 77

Scripture Index 78

Theme Index 78

Lessons for Any Occasion

Fire Prevention

THEME: *God will help us control our anger.*

SCRIPTURE: *"A gentle answer turns away wrath, but a harsh word stirs up anger" (Proverbs 15:1).*

"Likewise the tongue is a small part of the body, but it makes great boasts. Consider what a great forest is set on fire by a small spark" (James 3:5).

PREPARATION: *You will need a Bible, two books of matches, a foil-lined cake pan, and a cup of water. Place one book of matches in the pan, and set it aside.*

The Object Lesson

Think about a time you were really mad.
- What were you mad about?
- What did you do?

Anger can be a lot like a fire. *(Hold up a match.)* It kind of burns and makes us feel hot and mad. *(Light a match, and watch it burn.)* And just like fire, anger can hurt people. When you let your mad feelings continue burning inside you *(set the match in the pan on top of the book of matches so the book catches fire)*, it's likely that you'll say or do hurtful things to people around you. *(Pour the cup of water over the burning matches to put the fire out.)*
- What kind of things do you do when you feel "burning" mad?
- How do you think that makes others feel?

When you keep the "mad" alive, the fire inside you gets bigger and bigger, just like the fire in the pan. *(Read aloud James 3:5.)*
- What does this verse say about our angry words?

(Light another match.) Let's pretend this fire is another angry feeling.
- What could I do to keep this fire from getting out of control?
(Let a child blow out the flame.)
- What can you do to keep your angry feelings from getting out of control?

Being kind, loving, and forgiving are good ways to get rid of angry feelings. Even a smile or a hug can be like a bucket of water poured over those angry "flames" inside you. *(Read aloud Proverbs 15:1.)* In this passage, the word "wrath" means anger.
- How easy or difficult is it to use "gentle" words when you're angry?

● When you're mad, what might help you follow the advice in this verse?

It can be hard to be kind, loving, and forgiving when you feel hot and mad inside. But God will help you "blow out" the fire before it gets out of control. Let's pray and ask God to give us strength when we're mad.

Prayer

Dear God, thank you for the children you've brought here today. Help us extinguish our angry feelings so we won't hurt those around us. Give us the strength to be kind and loving. In Jesus' name, amen.

The Tools of the Trade

THEME: *The Bible is our guide.*

SCRIPTURE: *"All Scripture is God-breathed and is useful for teaching, rebuking, correcting and training in righteousness"* *(2 Timothy 3:16).*

PREPARATION: *You will need a Bible and a toolbox containing a hammer, a screwdriver, a tape measure, a pair of pliers, and a chisel.*

The Object Lesson

(Read 2 Timothy 3:16 aloud.)

● What does this passage tell us about the Bible?

God's Word helps us in many parts of our lives. Did you know that the Bible *(hold up your Bible)* is a lot like a toolbox? *(Point to the toolbox.)* Let me show you what I mean.

(Have a child hold up the hammer.)

● When your mom or dad pounds a nail into a wall, how many times does he or she have to hit the nail?

It's awfully hard to get a nail all the way into the wood with just one hit. And as Christians, we can't learn everything about God by reading the Bible one time. We have to keep reading and "hammering away" to learn how God wants us to live. Children and adults need to always keep learning.

(Have a child hold up the screwdriver.)

● What do you do with a screwdriver?

The screwdriver reminds us to **turn** to God when we're having a problem. When you turn the screwdriver, the screw goes deeper into the wood. And when we turn to God, we grow deeper in our love for him.

(Have a child hold up the tape measure.)

● What do you do with a tape measure?

When you're building something, it's important to measure your wood or other materials to be sure everything will line up correctly. Otherwise, your house might come out crooked! And a crooked house won't stand up very long.

The Bible is sort of like a tape measure, too. We can use it to measure our actions and words to be sure they line up with the way

God wants us to live. When you read God's Word, you'll learn the things God wants you to do and say.

(Have a child hold up the pliers.)

● What do people use pliers for?

Pliers help us get a good grip on things when our hands aren't strong enough. The Bible helps us hold on to God. By reading the Bible, we discover more about who God is, how much he loves us, and the way he expects us to live.

(Have a child hold up the chisel.)

This is a chisel. People use it to chip off extra rock or concrete that they don't need. Some artists use special chisels to carve beautiful statues. They need a chisel to knock away wood or stone and to shape the wood or stone into something new.

When we read the Bible, sometimes we discover that we have extra things in our lives—things such as jealousy, pride, or anger. The Bible shows us how to chisel these things away to create a beautiful, Christlike person.

(Point to the toolbox.) It's important to have a toolbox to build or fix things the right way. *(Hold up your Bible.)*

● Why is it important to have this "toolbox"?

● In what ways will the Bible make your life different?

God gave us a special toolbox when he gave us the Bible. Let's pray and thank God for giving us the tools we need to live for him.

Prayer

Dear God, thank you for the Bible. Thank you that we can study it and learn how you want us to live. Thank you for this wonderful tool that helps us grow closer to you. In Jesus' name, amen.

A Clear Connection

THEME: *Jesus is our link to God.*

SCRIPTURE: *"For there is one God and one mediator between God and men, the man Christ Jesus" (1 Timothy 2:5).*

PREPARATION: *You will need a Bible, tape, scissors, a marker, and construction paper. Use at least ten strips of construction paper (about 2x6 inches each) to create a paper chain. You'll also need one extra link with the word "Jesus" written on it.*

The Object Lesson

When you call someone on the telephone, you're connected through lots of telephone wires.

● What happens when the telephone wires get broken or damaged?

Sometimes it's hard to hear the person on the other end, or you might even get cut off completely! That reminds me of our relationship with God.

(Hold up the paper chain, and point to one end.) Let's pretend this link represents God. The link at the other end will represent us. God loves us and wants to be "linked" to us. But sometimes we do things that break or damage that connection.

● What things might hurt our "link" with God?

(Each time a child mentions a sinful action, tear one of the middle links and set the broken links aside.)

(Hold up the two ends of the chain.) Sometimes we lie instead of telling the truth. Sometimes we hate instead of loving others. Because of our sin—our wrong choices—our relationship with God gets broken.

● How can we fix our relationship so we can feel close to God again?

God made a way for us to fix our relationship with him. He gave us Jesus. *(Have a child read aloud 1 Timothy 2:5. Explain that the word "mediator" means someone who helps two people communicate. Then use the "Jesus" strip of paper as a link that joins the two ends of the chain and makes it complete again.)* When Jesus died, he paid for all the sins that hurt our relationship with God. When we believe in Jesus, we can be linked to God forever!

- Can sins still hurt our relationship with God?
- What can you do when you sin?

When we believe in Jesus, God forgives our sins. We can ask for his forgiveness to keep our "connection" strong.

Prayer

God, thank you so much for sending Jesus to be our link to you. Thank you for loving us so much that you want to have a relationship with us. Help us not to sin, so our connection with you will be clear and strong. In Jesus' name, amen.

Only One Way

THEME: *Jesus is the only way to heaven.*

SCRIPTURE: *"Jesus answered, 'I am the way and the truth and the life. No one comes to the Father except through me' "* *(John 14:6).*

PREPARATION: *You will need a Bible; individually wrapped candies; and a box (such as a toolbox or a tackle box) that is locked with a padlock, including the key to open the box. Inside the box, place an individually wrapped candy for each child.*

The Object Lesson

(Set the box where everyone can see it.) There's a special treat inside this box, but I can't seem to get the box open. Maybe if we're really good and extra nice, the box will open. Let's try saying "please."

(Lead children in saying "please" and then try to open the box.)

Maybe we should pat the box and tell it how nice it is.

(Lead children in patting the box and saying phrases such as "You're a really nice box" or "I really like you." Then try to open the box.)

- Why didn't our words and actions open the box?
- What are some other ways we could open the box?

We need a key, don't we? That's the only way to get the treat.

- What would we do if we didn't have this key?

There's a verse in the Bible that tells us about someone who is like a key. *(Read aloud John 14:6.)*

- How is Jesus like a key?
- What things do people do to try to reach heaven?
- How can you help others know about the key to heaven?

(Unlock the box, and give a treat to each child.) Just like this key was the only way to reach these treats, Jesus is the only way for us to be with God. People may try being good, doing nice things, or using kind words, but Jesus is the only way. Since there's only one way to heaven, it's important that we tell everyone it's Jesus.

Prayer

Jesus, thank you for each child here. Thank you that you are our key to heaven. Help us tell others that you are the only way. Amen.

Believin' Balloon-Blowers

THEME: *God helps us have faith in him.*

SCRIPTURE: *"Now faith is being sure of what we hope for and certain of what we do not see" (Hebrews 11:1).*

PREPARATION: *You will need a Bible and a large balloon (at least nine inches in diameter). Inflate the balloon, and tie it off.*

The Object Lesson

(Hold up the balloon.) We're going to try an experiment. Let's see if we can pass this balloon around our group without touching it. You may blow on the balloon to make it move. Ready?

(Let children pass the balloon by blowing on it. After the balloon has "traveled" to every child, retrieve the balloon and hold it in your lap.)

● What did you think of this experiment?

● Could you see anything that made the balloon move?

● How did you know that your breath was moving the balloon?

Usually it's hard to believe in things we can't see. But you could see the balloon moving, so you knew that your breath was working. This activity reminds me of a Bible verse. *(Read aloud Hebrews 11:1.)*

● What are some things you can't see but you have faith in?

● Why do you have faith in those things?

You had faith that your breath would move the balloon because you could see the balloon moving. We can have faith in God even though we can't see him, because we can see him working in our lives.

● How can you "see" God?

● Why does God want us to have faith in him?

When we have faith in God, he can use us to do great things. *(Hold up the balloon.)* Think of the way your invisible breath controlled this balloon. Even though we can't see God, we can have faith that he's in control of our lives. We also have faith that God hears our prayers, so let's pray and thank him right now.

Prayer

God, thank you for listening to us and always being near us, even though we can't see you. Help us have faith in you and believe that you're in control of our lives. Even when things seem scary, we want to put our faith in you. Amen.

Shiny and Clean

THEME: *God's forgiveness wipes away our sins.*

SCRIPTURE: *"Repent, then, and turn to God, that your sins may be wiped out" (Acts 3:19a).*

PREPARATION: *You will need a Bible, a tarnished penny, lemon juice, a baby-food jar (or another small container with a lid), salt, and a paper towel. Pour four tablespoons of lemon juice into the jar and then add two tablespoons of salt.*

The Object Lesson

(Hold up the tarnished penny.) This penny is pretty dirty.
● Should I throw it away?
● Do you think it's still valuable?

Even though the penny is dirty, it's still a penny and its value is the same. I'll put the penny in this jar while we talk a little more. *(Drop the penny in the jar, and close the lid tightly. Shake the jar while you continue talking.)*

The dirty penny reminds me of our lives when we sin.
● How do you feel when you do wrong things?
● Do you think God loves you even though you do wrong things?

Just as the dirty penny is still valuable, God still loves you just as much when you've sinned. But God wants our lives to be clean and new. *(Read aloud Acts 3:19a.)*

Repenting means telling God what we've done wrong and asking him to forgive us.
● What happens when we ask for God's forgiveness?

The Bible says that when we ask for God's forgiveness, he wipes away our sins and makes us clean again. *(Take the penny out of the jar and wipe it with the paper towel to reveal a bright and shiny penny.)*

(Hold up the penny.) Let's thank God for his love and forgiveness that takes away our sins and makes us shiny and clean.

Prayer

Dear God, you know that we sin and do wrong things. You know that sometimes our hearts are dirty with sin. Thank you for reminding us of the power of your love and forgiveness. In Jesus' name, amen.

God's Point of View

THEME: *We can trust in God's plan.*

SCRIPTURE: *"Trust in the Lord with all your heart and lean not on your own understanding; in all your ways acknowledge him, and he will make your paths straight"* (Proverbs 3:5-6).

PREPARATION: *You will need a Bible and a piece of embroidery or cross-stitch that has been completed but not mounted or framed.*

The Object Lesson

Think of a hard time you've been through. Maybe a pet died, or you had to move. Maybe you're having a hard time in school. *(Pause for children to think.)*

● Why do you think you had to go through that hard time?

It's hard to understand why we have to go through sad or frustrating situations. We know that God is powerful enough to stop those things from happening, but sometimes he chooses to let them happen. The Bible gives us good advice when we face hard times. *(Read aloud Proverbs 3:5-6.)*

● How can you show that you trust God?

● How do you think it feels to follow God's ways rather than your own?

Life is full of hard lessons that make us strong and help us trust God. Maybe this will show you what I mean.

(Hold up the needlework so children see the back side.) This side is how we sometimes see life.

● What does this look like?

Sometimes life doesn't make sense. Problems can make life confusing, frustrating, and even a little bit "ugly." But God has a plan! *(Point to the knots on the needlework.)* See all these knots? If this needlework didn't have knots, all the threads would pull out and we wouldn't have a pretty picture on the other side.

(Turn the picture over so children can see the picture.) The knots hold things together just like your faith in God holds you together and makes you strong.

Every stitch is in its place to create a beautiful picture. So the next time you don't understand why certain things happen, remember that God has a plan for everything to turn out for good.

Prayer

God, thank you for being in control and knowing everything about our lives. Help us to trust you and lean on your wisdom during hard times. Show us your good plans, and give us the strength to trust you when things are difficult in our lives. In Jesus' name, amen.

The Write Stuff

THEME: *Everyone in God's family is important.*

SCRIPTURE: *"Now you are the body of Christ, and each one of you is a part of it" (1 Corinthians 12:27).*

PREPARATION: *You will need a Bible, index cards, and a ballpoint pen (the kind that has a spring in it that can be taken apart).*

The Object Lesson

(Give each child an index card. Then take the pen apart, and distribute the pieces among the children. If you have a large group, you may need more than one pen. Ask each child to sign his or her name on the card with his or her piece of the pen. Allow children to react for a moment and then collect the pen pieces and cards.)

- Why can't you write with your piece of the pen?
- Why is your part important to make the pen work?

Just as I gave you different parts of a pen, God has given each of us an important job to do. And just as all the parts of the pen have to work together, we must work together to accomplish God's plans.

(Read aloud 1 Corinthians 12:27.)

- What jobs do people do to make a church service run smoothly?

(Children may mention tasks such as printing the bulletin, practicing music, taking care of babies in the nursery, teaching, and cleaning the church.)

- What might happen if some people didn't do their jobs?

(Hold up the pen pieces.) Remember the spring in the pen? It's a part that we can't even see when the pen is working properly. But the pen won't work at all without it. All the pieces have to work together.

(Put the pen back together, and write "God loves you" on an index card.)

Prayer

Dear God, thank you for reminding us that everyone is important to you. Help us work together and do our special jobs so others may learn about you, too. Amen.

Lending Us a Hand

THEME: *The Holy Spirit is our helper.*

SCRIPTURE: *"For it is God who works in you to will and to act according to his good purpose" (Philippians 2:13).*

PREPARATION: *You will need a Bible and a glove.*

The Object Lesson

- When is it hard for you to obey?
- What happens when you don't obey?

Sometimes it's hard to obey our parents or teachers. It can also be hard to obey God. But God's commands are the ones we need to obey more than anything! That's why God has given us a helper—the Holy Spirit. When you become a Christian, the Holy Spirit lives in you to help you obey God. Let me show you what I mean.

(Lay a Bible in front of you where children can see it. Set the glove beside the Bible.)

Glove, pick up the Bible, go pat [child's name] on the back, and be kind to him [her].

- Why won't the glove obey me?
- What would help the glove obey my commands?

(Put your hand in the glove.) Just as the glove needs a hand to help it obey, you and I need the Holy Spirit to help us obey God's commands. Now, glove—pick up the Bible *(pick up the Bible)*, and go pat [child's name] on the back. *(Pat a child on the back.)*

When it's hard to obey and do what's right, remember—the Holy Spirit lives in you and helps you. Let's thank God for giving us the Holy Spirit.

Prayer

God, thank you for sending a helper—the Holy Spirit—to help us obey your commands. Show us how to hear and obey so we can be faithful followers. In Jesus' name, amen.

Puzzle Presents

THEME: *We all have important spiritual gifts.*

SCRIPTURE: *"There are different kinds of gifts, but the same Spirit. There are different kinds of service, but the same Lord" (1 Corinthians 12:4-5).*

PREPARATION: *You will need a Bible and a child's puzzle with enough pieces for each child in your group to have one. (If you have more than fifteen children in your group, have children form pairs and share puzzle pieces.)*

The Object Lesson

(Give each child a puzzle piece, and let children look at their pieces.)
● If we put our pieces together, what would the picture look like?
● Why is it hard to tell exactly what the picture would look like?
(Let children work together to assemble the puzzle. You may need to encourage children to start with the edge pieces and then "build" pieces into the middle. Be sure everyone can see the finished picture.)
● What would have happened if we left out someone's piece?
● Are any of these puzzle pieces more important than the others?
Without even one of the pieces, our picture would be incomplete. God's family is a lot like this puzzle. God gives each person special gifts or talents—things that person can do really well.
● What talents or gifts do some people have?
● How can they use those talents to serve God?
Some people can sing well; others know how to teach or tell stories. Some people love to care for babies, while others enjoy working with teenagers. The Bible tells us that each of those gifts is important. *(Read aloud 1 Corinthians 12:4-5.)*
You couldn't tell what the picture was just by looking at one piece. That's why God gave each person a special gift—our gifts can fit to- gether with others' gifts and create a beautiful picture of his love!

Prayer

God, thank you that each child here is important to you and has a special job to do for you. Help us use our gifts and talents to serve you and show others your love. In Jesus' name, amen.

Vegetable Variety

THEME: *God made each person unique.*

SCRIPTURE: *"So in Christ we who are many form one body, and each member belongs to all the others. We have different gifts, according to the grace given us" (Romans 12:5-6a).*

PREPARATION: *You will need a Bible, a Crock-Pot full of warm vegetable soup, and a large spoon.*

The Object Lesson

(Take the lid off the pot, and let children smell the soup. Stir the soup so children can see what kinds of vegetables are in it.)
- What do you think makes this soup smell so good?
- Which ingredient do you think is the most important?
- What would the soup be like if I used just one ingredient?

It takes lots of different vegetables, cooked together, to create the yummy taste and smell of vegetable soup. Each vegetable adds a different flavor. It's that variety that makes vegetable soup so tasty. Did you know that God's family is a little like vegetable soup? Let me show you how.

(Read aloud Romans 12:5-6a.)
- How do you think God's family is like vegetable soup?
- What if everyone was exactly the same? What would that be like?

God made each of us unique, with different talents, likes, dislikes, and interests. When all of us work together, doing the different things God asks us to do, we make a wonderful church. If we were all the same, our church would be kind of dull...just like a pot full of carrots would be kind of dull. Let's thank God for "stirring up" a fantastic blend of people! *(Depending on your situation, you may want to give children each a sample of the vegetable soup.)*

Prayer

Thank you, God for all of the different people you created. Thank you that we're all unique, each with special gifts and talents to serve you. Help us to love others and to appreciate the special way you've made them. Amen.

No Call-Waiting

THEME: *God hears us.*

SCRIPTURE: *"They will call on my name and I will answer them" (Zechariah 13:9b).*

PREPARATION: *You will need a Bible. (Optional: Cut telephones out of construction paper, and print the verse on them. Give one to each child to use as a bookmark.)*

The Object Lesson

● Have you ever tried to call your mom or dad or grandma but you only heard "beep, beep, beep"?

● What does that sound mean?

● Do you like having to wait and try again?

● What if you call and no one answers, but you get a machine telling you to leave a message? Is that the same thing as talking to the person?

● How do you feel if no one answers at all?

It can be hard to get ahold of people sometimes. But listen to this message from God! *(Read aloud Zechariah 13:9b.)*

● According to this verse, will God ever give you a "busy signal"?

● Will God ask you to leave a message?

This Scripture says that God will hear us. It doesn't say that God is busy or "on another line." It doesn't ask us to leave a message. God will hear us!

● How do we talk to God?

When you pray, you can be sure God hears you—no matter where you are or when you "call." God wants to hear everything you have to say! He's never too busy, and he's always listening. Let's talk to God right now!

Prayer

Dear God, thank you for always having time for us. It's nice to know that you're always listening and will never ask us to leave a message or "call" later. Thank you for loving us so much that you want to hear what we have to say. We love you, too. Amen.

Heavy Hearts

THEME: *Jesus lifts our burdens.*

SCRIPTURE: *"Come to me, all you who are weary and burdened, and I will give you rest" (Matthew 11:28).*

PREPARATION: *You will need a Bible and several heavy objects, such as books, ankle weights, or a six-pack of soda.*

The Object Lesson

I need some helpers to hold these items for me. *(Call several volunteers, and give each child one item to hold over his or her head while you talk. To speed up the effect, you may ask children to hold their items with one hand.)*

● How do you think our volunteers' arms feel?

● When have you felt tired or worn-out?

Carrying heavy things, running, or exercising are things that make our bodies feel tired. People also feel tired or weary when they carry heavy things like sin or sadness with them.

● How is sin or sadness like a heavy burden?

Jesus doesn't want us carrying our sins, worries, or sorrows with us. Listen to what he said. *(Read aloud Matthew 11:28.)*

● What does Jesus want us to do with our burdens?

(Have the children who are holding the "burdens" set them down.

● How did it feel to set down your burden?

● How do you think it would feel to give Jesus your sins, worries, and sorrows?

When we ask God to forgive our sins or trust God with our worries, it's as if that heavy load is lifted off our shoulders. Jesus wants to give us rest from those burdens that make our lives heavy. He wants us to feel light and joyful. Let's praise Jesus for lifting our burdens.

(If time allows, let each child have a turn holding a heavy object over his or her head for a few seconds.)

Prayer

Dear Jesus, thank you for giving us rest from things like sin and sadness. Thank you for dying on the cross to take those things away. Help us give our burdens to you so we can find rest. Amen.

Rise Above It

THEME: *God helps us overcome hard times.*

SCRIPTURE: *"Never will I leave you; never will I forsake you (Hebrews 13:5b).*

PREPARATION: *You will need a Bible, two loaves of frozen bread-dough, two loaf pans, and two dish towels. One loaf needs to be thawed, but it should not have risen much. The other loaf needs to be thawed and must have risen significantly. Place each loaf in a loaf pan, and cover both pans with dish towels.*

The Object Lesson

- Have you ever helped someone bake bread?
- What do you have to do to the dough?

To make bread light and fluffy, you have to treat the dough a little roughly! *(Hold up the unrisen dough, and demonstrate how to knead it.)* To make sure all the ingredients are mixed together, it's important to knead the dough—that means pushing it, mushing it, pulling it, and digging into it. Sometimes you even have to punch the dough down! *(Place the dough in the pan.)*

- What are some situations that make us feel "punched down"?
- What do you do when things push and pull at you?

Things in life can make us feel punched down or discouraged. But God tells us in Hebrews 13:5b, "Never will I leave you; never will I forsake you." That means that God will help us through hard times.

In fact, when we love and follow Jesus *(lift the towel from the risen dough to show children how "big" it is)*, we can rise above those hard times. This dough has yeast in it—that's what makes the dough rise and fill with little pockets of air. When Jesus is our friend, he fills us with joy to help us overcome sadness, anger, or frustration.

Let's thank God right now for being with us—through life's punches!

Prayer

Jesus, we're glad to know that you never leave us or forsake us. Thank you for helping us through all the hard times that make us feel punched down. Help us rise above any situation. Amen.

mportant Instructions

THEME: *The Bible shows us the way.*

SCRIPTURE: *"Your word is a lamp to my feet and a light for my path" (Psalm 119:105).*

PREPARATION: *You will need a Bible, a dress pattern, a cookbook, a road map, and an owner's manual for any appliance.*

The Object Lesson

(Choose four volunteers to hold up the pattern, the cookbook, the road map, and the owner's manual.)

● What are each of these items used for?

● What might happen if a cook didn't use a cookbook or a seamstress didn't use a pattern?

● Why would someone choose not to use one of these things?

All of these items give important instructions. Imagine how awful a special dessert might taste if your mom or dad didn't use a cookbook. And you can get lost if you don't use a map when you're traveling in a strange place.

(Collect the items, and bring out the Bible.) I brought another important instruction manual.

● How do the instructions in the Bible help us?

● What might happen if we try to live without reading **these** important instructions?

This is our instruction manual from God. One verse describes God's Word this way. *(Read aloud Psalm 119:105.)*

● How is God's Word like a light or a lamp?

The Bible is an important instruction manual that shows us how to live, follow God, love others, and believe in Jesus. God gave us this special book to guide us when life gets dark or confusing. We'd be lost without it!

Prayer

Dear God, thank you for your special instruction manual—the Bible. Help us to read your Word every day to show us the way to live. We want to follow you and obey your instructions. In Jesus' name, amen.

Lessons in Life

THEME: *Jesus helps us face challenges.*

SCRIPTURE: *"In this world you will have trouble. But take heart! I have overcome the world" (John 16:33b).*

PREPARATION: *You will need a Bible; a paper bag; and items such as a fork, a spoon, a pair of shoes with laces, a pencil, a shirt with buttons, a manual can-opener, a ruler, a book, and a comb. (You'll need one item per child.) Place the items in the bag.*

The Object Lesson

I've brought a few things that most of us have had to learn how to use. We may have learned a long time ago, or we may have learned just recently. I'll pass the bag around and let each person take out an item. When you choose your item, tell us what you remember about learning to use that item. You might recall that it was really hard to learn to tie your shoes or that you learned to comb your hair very quickly.

(Let the children take turns choosing objects from the bag and discussing the difficulties they had learning to use each one.)

You've learned to do lots of things. These challenges may have seemed difficult at first, but little by little, you kept trying and you finally got it! Now it probably seems simple to use your fork instead of your hands.

● What challenges do you think you'll face in the future?

As you grow up, you'll face new challenges. You'll have to learn to drive, do your taxes, write term papers, and other important things. Some things will be difficult, and others won't be so hard to learn.

Jesus knew we'd face challenges and difficulties. This is what he said. *(Read aloud John 16:33b.)*

● What is Jesus telling us in this verse?

● How does it feel to know that Jesus is more powerful than your difficulties?

● Now that you've heard this verse, what will you do when you face a challenge or a problem?

Jesus knew that we'd face hard things in life. He wanted to reassure us that he's more powerful than any problem we have. We can trust in Jesus to help us through all the hard times we face.

Prayer

Dear Jesus, we're glad that you are more powerful than any problem. Help us trust in you when we're facing something new and difficult. Give us the strength to overcome our problems. Amen.

The Most Wonderful Gift

THEME: *God gives his grace freely.*

SCRIPTURE: *"For it is by grace you have been saved, through faith—and this is not of yourself, it is the gift of God—not by works, so that no one can boast" (Ephesians 2:8-9).*

PREPARATION: *You will need a Bible and one treat (such as a piece of candy, a sticker, or a small toy) for each child.*

The Object Lesson

- When do you receive presents?
- Who gives them to you?
- Why do people give you gifts?

I've brought a special gift for each child today. *(Give each child a treat.)*

- What did you have to do to receive this gift?
- Why do you think I gave it to you?

You didn't have to earn this gift or even wait for a holiday to get it. I gave it to you because I like you! I also wanted to help you understand a special gift God gave to all of us. *(Read aloud Ephesians 2:8-9.)*

- What gift did God give us?

This verse tells us about God's free gift of grace—his love and forgiveness. God offers his love and forgiveness because he wants us to live with him in heaven.

- What do we have to do to receive grace?

There's nothing we can do to earn God's gift—we just have to accept it.

- How did you show that you wanted the gift I gave you?
- How can you show that you've accepted God's gift?

When you believe in Jesus, you're accepting God's love and forgiveness. And that's a gift we all need!

Prayer

Dear God, thank you for your free gift of love and forgiveness. Thank you for loving us so much that you sent Jesus to pay for our sins. We know that there's nothing we can do to earn your love. Help us to accept it as a free gift. In Jesus' name, amen.

Cracked Jars

THEME: *God can use us.*

SCRIPTURE: *"Moses answered, 'What if they do not believe me or listen to me and say, "The Lord did not appear to you"?' " (Exodus 4:1).*

PREPARATION: *You will need a potted plant or flower and a jar with a crack or a chip in it. Fill the jar with water.*

The Object Lesson

This plant needs water, or it'll die. But the only water I have is in this old, cracked jar. I can't use this to water my plant. This jar isn't good enough!

- What will happen if I don't water the plant?
- Even though the jar is old and broken, can it help the plant stay alive?
- Which is more important, the jar or the water inside it?

Water is water! It doesn't make any difference what kind of container it's in. This reminds me of a Bible story about Moses. Because Moses couldn't speak very well, he didn't think he was good enough to carry God's message to the people. He thought the people wouldn't listen to him.

Just like the plant needed water, the people needed to hear God's special message. And just like the old jar would do a fine job of watering, Moses was the person God wanted to deliver that message. God has important things for us to do, too.

- How should you respond when God asks you to do something?
- What might keep you from doing what God asks?

Sometimes we feel like we're too small or too young to do important things for God. But God can use all of us—even when we feel like this old, cracked jar. As long as we trust him and listen to him, we can do anything God asks us to do.

(Let a child water the plant.)

Prayer

Dear God, thank you for using us just as we are. Help us to trust you and obey when you have a special job for us to do. Amen.

This Little Light

THEME: *Our actions show God's love.*

SCRIPTURE: *"Neither do people light a lamp and put it under a bowl. Instead they put it on its stand, and it gives light to everyone in the house" (Matthew 5:15).*

PREPARATION: *You will need a Bible, a flashlight, and a small basket such as a waste-paper basket. Before the lesson, darken the meeting area as much as possible.*

The Object Lesson

(Lead children in singing "This Little Light of Mine.")
- What light is this song referring to?
- Why is it important to shine that light?

This song comes from a passage in the Bible. *(Read aloud Matthew 5:15.)* Let's see if we can discover what the author of this passage was talking about.

(Turn on the flashlight, and hold it in front of you.)
- How can this flashlight help me in a dark room?

(Have a child place the basket over the light.)
- Is the flashlight very useful to us now? Explain.
- Why would I want to have the basket placed over the light?

(Turn off the flashlight, and turn on the room lights.)

The Bible tells us that sin has made our lives dark and dirty. But when we have Jesus' love inside us, our lives are different. When we show Jesus' love to people around us, it's like shining a light into a dark world. God doesn't want us to hide our actions or stop telling people about Jesus. That would be like putting a basket over this light!

- What can you do to shine Jesus' love to people around you?

Let's pray and ask God to help us be lights in a dark world.

Prayer

Dear Jesus, we're glad that you take away the sin and darkness in our lives. Help us to shine your love to people around us, so they can know the joy of living in your light. Give us the courage to tell people about you instead of hiding our lights. Amen.

Kindness Trees (Week One)

(Note: This lesson takes two sessions.)

THEME: God wants us to show kindness to others.

SCRIPTURE: "Be kind and compassionate to one another, forgiving each other, just as in Christ God forgave you" (Ephesians 4:32).

PREPARATION: You will need a Bible, crayons or markers, and white paper. Color simple tree-trunks on sheets of white paper. You will need one paper with a tree trunk on it for each child.

The Object Lesson

God gives us lots of special instructions on how to treat others. (Read aloud Ephesians 4:32.)
- What are ways you can show kindness?
- Why do you think God wants us to be kind to others?

There's another passage in the Bible that tells us why it's important to be kind. Listen and see if you can find why we should be kind. (Read aloud Matthew 25:34-40.)
- Why is it important to be kind to others?

The Bible says that when we show kindness to people, it's just like showing kindness to God. That's pretty important!

Today we are going to start a week-long experiment. (Distribute the paper tree-trunks.) These are "Kindness Trees."
- What's wrong with these trees?

Our Kindness Trees need to grow some leaves. And Kindness Trees can only grow leaves when an act of kindness has been done. Take your tree home, and hang it where you will be sure to see it every day. Each time you're kind to someone, draw a leaf on your tree. If you're kind to someone and you keep it a secret, add two leaves. It's extra special to do secret acts of kindness! I'd like to see your trees next time we meet, so bring them with you. We'll see how your trees grew!

Prayer

Dear God, thank you for your love and kindness to us each day. Help us show kindness to others through our actions and words. Remind us that everything we do for others, we're doing for you. Amen.

Kindness Trees (Week Two)

THEME: *God helps us to show kindness to others.*

SCRIPTURE: *"Be kind and compassionate to one another, forgiving each other, just as in Christ God forgave you"* (Ephesians 4:32).

PREPARATION: *You will need a Bible and a Kindness Tree (from last week's lesson) with several leaves drawn on it.*

The Object Lesson

Last week we talked about kindness.

● What do you remember about our lesson?

Let's look again at what God's Word tells us about kindness. *(Read aloud Ephesians 4:32.)* If you brought your Kindness Tree today, hold it up high. *(Hold up the sample tree you've brought.)* Some of your trees really grew!

● What did you do to make your trees grow?

● How did it feel to do those things?

● How do you think other people felt when you were kind to them?

No two trees grew the same way, did they? Everyone did different acts of kindness, and no action was better than any other. All of your acts of kindness made these trees beautiful!

● Your trees sure changed a lot in a week. Do you think you changed at all? Explain.

When you're kind and loving, you're showing God's love to others. That's what God wants us to do—that's how he uses us to make his family grow! Your Kindness Trees can keep on growing, too. You may want to add more leaves or make a new tree each week. Even if you don't, you'll notice a big change when you're kind to others!

Prayer

God, thank you for the ways these children showed love and kindness this week. Help them to continue growing in you as they spread your love to those around them. In Jesus' name, amen.

The Recipe for Life

THEME: *We can trust God.*

SCRIPTURE: *"As the heavens are higher than the earth, so are my ways higher than your ways and my thoughts than your thoughts" (Isaiah 55:9).*

PREPARATION: *You will need a Bible, a sack of flour, and enough homemade cookies or brownies for each child to have one. (Note: If you don't have time to bake, it's OK to bring store-bought cookies. Simply change the wording of the lesson to indicate that someone else made the cookies.)*

The Object Lesson

(Hold up the sack of flour.) I baked something last night, and this is one of the ingredients I used.

- What do you think I made?
- Why can't you tell me what it is?
- What would help you know for sure what I baked last night?

It would be almost impossible for you to know what I made, since I only showed you one ingredient. Let's see if this helps. *(Bring out the cookies, and give one to each child.)*

- What other ingredients did I need to make these treats?
- Are all of the ingredients important? Explain.

It takes lots of ingredients to make these cookies—things like flour, sugar, eggs, and butter. If you looked at each ingredient separately, you'd never know what the final product—the cookies—was going to be.

Each situation in your life is sort of like an ingredient. It's as if God is following a recipe to create a wonderful person in each of us. Some of the ingredients are sad.

- What are some things that have made you sad?

Some ingredients are happy.

- What things in life have made you happy?

We can't understand God's plans for us by just looking at one situation, or ingredient. In Isaiah 55:9, God says, "As the heavens are higher than the earth, so are my ways higher than your ways and my thoughts than your thoughts."

- What does that mean?

God has special plans for all of us. And God's plans require a certain blend of "ingredients." Even though we may not understand why we have to go through each situation, we can trust that God is using those things to create something wonderful.

Prayer

God, thank you for creating something wonderful in each of our lives. Help us to trust you when the "ingredients" are confusing or make us sad. We know that your ways aren't like ours, so show us how to put our faith in you. In Jesus' name, amen.

The Real Thing

THEME: *It's important to test other teachings.*

SCRIPTURE: *"Dear friends, do not believe every spirit, but test the spirits to see whether they are from God, because many false prophets have gone out into the world. This is how you can recognize the Spirit of God: Every spirit that acknowledges that Jesus Christ has come in the flesh is from God" (1 John 4:1-2).*

PREPARATION: *You will need a Bible, a real dollar bill, and a toy dollar bill. (Optional: You may want to provide a toy dollar for each child to take home.)*

The Object Lesson

(Hold out the toy dollar.) I brought a dollar bill today so you could help me decide how to spend it.

- What do you think I should spend my money on?
- Why would I have trouble buying anything with this dollar?
- How do you know that this isn't a real dollar?

You know what a real dollar looks like, so it's easy for you to spot a fake. *(Get out a real dollar, and hold the two bills side by side.)*

- How are these two dollars different?
- What might happen if I tried to spend the fake one?

It's important to know the real thing so no one can mislead you with something false. That's true with dollars, but it's more important when it comes to Jesus.

- What are some true things you know about Jesus?
- What are some untrue things people might say about Jesus?

There are many people who listen to lies and follow false teachings about God or Jesus. We could study those teachings to know why they're false, just as we could study lots of fake dollars to know what's wrong with them. Let's see what the Bible tells us to do. *(Read aloud 1 John 4:1-2.)*

- What does this passage tell us to do?

When we're not sure if someone is telling the truth about God or Jesus, the Bible tells us to simply compare everything to God's Word. We don't have to study other teachings to see if they are real. If we know the truth about Jesus, we'll be able to spot any false teachings.

(Hold up the real dollar.) God's Word is the real thing. *(Hold up the toy dollar.)* Anything else is just a fake!

Prayer

Dear Jesus, thank you for being the real thing—someone we can trust and believe in. Give us wisdom to know when people try to lead us away from you with false teachings. Help us understand the Bible so we can compare other teachings with yours. Amen.

Flex Your Faith

THEME: *We can build our faith by putting it to work.*

SCRIPTURE: *"In the same way, faith by itself, if it is not accompanied by action, is dead" (James 2:17).*

PREPARATION: *You will need a Bible and a few small dumbbells or hand weights.*

The Object Lesson

(Hold up the weights.)
- What are these?
- Why do people use them?
- What would it take for me to move from lifting these little weights to lifting something much heavier?

A person has to practice a long time to build strong muscles. It takes a lot of time and hard work. I'm not sure if I'm up for all that—it sounds tiring!

- If **you** lifted weights, would I get strong muscles? Explain.

If **you** did all the work, **I** wouldn't get any stronger. Lifting weights is a lot like having faith in God. In order to have a strong faith, we have to put it to work. We have to test our faith and use our faith so it will get stronger.

(Read aloud James 2:17.)

- Why does God want us to show that we have faith in him or that we trust him?
- What are specific ways you can show that you believe in God?
- Will my faith get stronger if you do those things for me? Explain.

God wants our faith in him to grow strong. But that only comes by loving and trusting God, believing in his Word, and doing our best to follow his commands. No one else can do those things for you. Let's ask God to help us strengthen our faith.

Prayer

Dear God, help us as we try to strengthen our faith in you. Show us ways to demonstrate our belief in you and our love for you. Thank you for loving us. Amen.

I Just Can't Wait

THEME: *We can look forward to heaven.*

SCRIPTURE: *"But in keeping with his promise we are looking forward to a new heaven and a new earth, the home of righteousness" (2 Peter 3:13).*

PREPARATION: *You will need a Bible, a seed catalog, and a small planter in which you've planted any seed. The seed catalog should have a picture of the plant your seed will become.*

The Object Lesson

I've brought something special to show you. *(Show children the potted seed.)* I'm excited about the tiny seed that's buried here.

● Why do you think I'm excited about this?

● What do you think this little seed might grow up to be?

This planted seed may not look exciting or interesting, because you can't see what it's going to be. *(Bring out the seed catalog, and show children the picture of what the seed will grow to look like.)* Even though the little seed doesn't look like much now, the seed company promises that this little seed will become a flower (or a vegetable).

● What's it like to wait for something good to happen?

It can be hard to wait for good things—just like it's hard to wait for a seed to grow into a plant. God has promised us something that we can really look forward to. *(Read aloud 2 Peter 3:13.)*

● What has God promised us?

● Why is that something we can look forward to?

God has promised that people who believe in Jesus will have a beautiful home in heaven where they'll live with him forever. And just as the seed is a promise of a plant to come, God's Word gives a promise of heaven to come. The more we learn about heaven, the more we'll look forward to being there with God. Let's thank God right now for the special place he's prepared for us.

Prayer

Dear God, thank you for preparing such a wonderful place for us in heaven. We're looking forward to spending forever with you in that special place. In Jesus' name, amen.

Only a Shell

THEME: *Death is only the beginning of life with God.*

SCRIPTURE: *"Jesus answered him, 'I tell you the truth, today you will be with me in paradise' " (Luke 23:43).*

PREPARATION: *You will need a Bible and an unshelled peanut.*

The Object Lesson

(Hold up the unshelled peanut.)
● What is this?
(Gently break open the shell, trying to keep part of it intact as a "hinge." Shake the peanut from its shell and then press the broken shell back together. Hold out the peanut.)
● What is this?
You just told me that this other piece was a peanut.
● How are the two pieces different?
● Does a peanut taste like a peanut because of its shell? What part makes a peanut taste so good?
We're a lot like this peanut. The part of you that everyone sees—your body—is sort of like the peanut shell. It doesn't give you a sense of humor, or help you love, or help you feel happy or sad. That part is inside of you, and it's called your soul. Your soul is kind of like the peanut inside its shell—it makes you who you are.
● Which part is more important to God—your body or your soul? Explain.
God loves every part of us. Our bodies are important—after all, God created them! But our souls are more important to God. That's the part of us that can love God, praise him, and obey him. That's the part of us that will live with God in heaven. Listen to what Jesus told a man just before the man was going to die.
(Read aloud Luke 23:43.)
● Do you think Jesus meant that the man's body would be in heaven? Explain.
(Hold up the peanut shell.) When we die, our "shell" stays here be-cause we don't need it anymore. *(Hold up the peanut.)* When people who believe in Jesus die, their souls go to heaven where they'll live with God forever. Death may mean the end of life in our bodies, but it's just the beginning of life with God!

Prayer

God, thank you for creating special bodies for us to live in while we're here on earth. Thank you for giving each person a soul that makes him or her able to love you. And most of all, thank you for making a wonderful place where we can live with you forever. In Jesus' name, amen.

Inside Out Love

THEME: *Love others for who they are.*

SCRIPTURE: *"The Lord does not look at the things man looks at. Man looks at the outward appearance, but the Lord looks at the heart" (I Samuel 16:7b).*

PREPARATION: *You will need a Bible.*

The Object Lesson

● How would you describe yourself so that a stranger could walk into the room and know who you were?

● Do you ever wish that you looked different than you do? Explain.

● Does the way people look affect the amount of love and kindness that you show them?

God created each person to look a certain way. And even though people are all different, each person is just as special and important as the next one. There's a passage in the Bible that talks about people being different from each other. *(Read aloud James 2:1-5.)*

● Have you ever treated someone differently because of the way he or she looked? Explain.

● How do you think people feel when you do that?

● Does Jesus love people because of the way they look? Explain.

God wants us to love people the way he does. The Bible says, "The Lord does not look at the things man looks at. Man looks at the outward appearance, but the Lord looks at the heart."

● What does this verse mean?

● How can you "look at the hearts" of people around you?

When we look at people's hearts, we're looking at people the way God does. And when we love people because of who they are rather than because of the way they look or what they wear, we're loving people the way God does.

Prayer

Dear God, thank you for making everyone special and unique. Help us to look at people's hearts rather than at their outer appearances. Show us how to love people the way you do. Amen.

Two Sides of Love

THEME: *Discipline is an important part of love.*

SCRIPTURE: *"Children [are] a reward from [the Lord]" (Psalm 127:3b).*

"He who spares the rod hates his son, but he who loves him is careful to discipline him" (Proverbs 13:24).

PREPARATION: *You will need a Bible and a rose with a thorny stem.*

The Object Lesson

- How would you describe love?
- Who are some people that love you?
- What do they do to make you feel loved?

Your parents love you because you are a gift from God. In fact, the Bible tells us in Psalm 127 that children are a reward from God. God gave you to your parents as a precious gift. That makes you very special! The love that your parents have for you is like a rose. *(Hold up the rose, and let children smell it and gently touch its petals.)*

- How do the rose petals feel?
- How should you treat rose petals?

The rose petals are very tender and beautiful. We have to treat them gently to take care of them. That's like one kind of love your parents have for you—a gentle, soft, and sweet love. *(Point to the thorns.)* These thorns remind me of another way your parents show that they love you. *(Let children touch the thorns.)*

- What do the thorns feel like?
- Why do you think God put sharp thorns on the rose?

God knew that some animals would like eating the tender rose petals. So he placed thorns on the rose to help protect it. The thorns might be unpleasant for us, but without them, the rose could easily die. Sometimes your parents have to show their love for you in unpleasant ways, too. That's called discipline.

- What happens when you go out to play instead of cleaning your room?
- What would your parents do if you hit your brother or sister?

When you do wrong things, your parents have to discipline you. The Bible tells us that discipline is important. *(Read aloud Proverbs 13:24.)*

- What might happen if your parents let you do whatever you wanted?
- How does discipline show that your parents love you?

It can be hard for parents to discipline their children—they'd rather have fun with you. But parents know that it's important for you to learn to follow rules and get along with other people. Just as the thorns protect the rose, your parents' discipline protects you from doing wrong things that could hurt you. *(Hold up the rose.)*

- What would the rose be like without thorns?
- What would the rose be like without petals?

If the rose didn't have thorns, it could be easily destroyed. If it was all thorns, it would just be a thorn bush. The rose needs both parts to grow and be beautiful. In the same way, children need both kinds of love to grow into wonderful adults! So the next time your parents discipline you, you can thank them for showing their love.

Prayer

Dear God, thank you for parents who love us with gentleness and with discipline. Thank you that the Bible helps our parents make wise choices. Even though it's hard to be disciplined, help us understand that our parents are doing it out of love. Amen.

Where a Flower Gets Its Power

THEME: *Abiding in Christ gives us power to do his work.*

SCRIPTURE: *"I am the vine; you are the branches. If a man remains in me and I in him, he will bear much fruit; apart from me you can do nothing" (John 15:5).*

PREPARATION: *You will need a Bible and a potted plant with several flowers or leaves.*

The Object Lesson

(Hold up the potted plant so children can see the flowers.)

• What things in this pot help the flowers (or leaves) to grow?

• What would happen to the flowers (or leaves) if I broke them off from the plant?

(Break off a flower or a leaf close to the point where it meets the plant.) This flower (or leaf) won't live very long away from the plant, the soil, and the water. *(Show children the end of the stem, where the flower or leaf was broken from the plant.)* You can see that this is where the flower (or leaf) got all the nutrients and "food" that helped it to grow. Without those things, the flower (or leaf) will shrivel up and die. *(Set the flower or leaf aside.)* There's a passage in the Bible that reminds me of this plant and flower (or leaf). Jesus was talking to his disciples, and this is what he said.

(Read aloud John 15:5.)

• How does this passage remind you of our plant and flower (or leaf)?

• If Jesus is like the plant and we're like the flowers, what important "food" does Jesus give us?

• What "fruit" does Jesus want us to produce?

Jesus wants us to understand that our relationship with him is important. He wants us to tell other people about God's love, so they can join God's family. And Jesus wants our friendship with God to grow closer every day. That's part of what it means to "bear fruit."

(Point to a healthy stem that's connected to the plant.) Just as this stem has to be connected to the plant in order to produce flowers, we have to be "connected" to Jesus in order to bear fruit.

● What can you do to stay connected to Jesus?

Prayer is a great way to stay close to Jesus. Let's pray and ask God to help us produce good fruit for him.

Prayer

Dear Jesus, we know that without you we can do nothing. We want to stay connected to you so we can help others know about God's love. Help us to be faithful in prayer, praise, and in studying your Word. Thank you for loving us and using us to tell others about God. Amen.

Cool Your Heels

THEME: *God wants us to have patience as we trust in him.*

SCRIPTURE: *"Wait for the Lord; be strong and take heart and wait for the Lord (Psalm 27:14).*

PREPARATION: *You will need a Bible and any frozen dessert that must be thawed before serving. Keep the dessert frozen for this lesson. (Note: You may want to have another dessert prepared to serve kids at the end of this lesson.)*

The Object Lesson

I brought a yummy snack for you today.
- Who would enjoy a big piece of dessert?

I love dessert, and I couldn't wait to enjoy it with you! But it's a frozen dessert, and I forgot to take it out of the freezer to thaw. It's still frozen, but I really want to eat it right now! I'm hungry! Let's see if we can eat it anyway.

(Bring out the frozen dessert, and let children look at it.)
- What would it be like to eat this dessert right now?
- What would it be like to eat this dessert when it's thawed?

(Set the dessert aside.) It can be hard to wait for good things.
- What things do you have a hard time waiting for?
- Why do we have to wait for those things?

Christmas, your birthday, a special vacation, or even a tasty treat are all things we'd like to have right now! But each of those things has a special time and place that they need to happen. Other things in life are hard to wait for, too—like when a parent is looking for a job, or a friend is very sick, or your family is going through a hard time. When those things happen, we want God to make them better right away. Let's see what the Bible says.

(Read aloud Psalm 27:14.)
- What does this verse tell you to do during hard times?
- Do you think it would be hard or easy to follow this Scripture? Explain.
- How might this verse help you during a hard time?

(Point to the dessert.) If I eat the dessert without waiting for it to thaw, I'll end up gnawing on an icy block! But if I follow the directions and wait for the dessert to thaw, I can enjoy something warm

and tasty. God wants us to follow his directions and wait for his plans, too. When we're facing a hard time, it can be hard to wait for God to take action. But he'll give us strength and peace to help us through until the time is right.

Prayer

Dear God, we're glad that you have special plans for our lives. We know that some of those plans might involve hard times or sadness. Give us strength to wait for your direction. Give us your peace to help us through the hard times. Help us wait for your timing. In Jesus' name, amen.

Ring Around My Heart

THEME: *God's love never ends.*

SCRIPTURE: *"For I am convinced that neither death nor life, neither angels nor demons, neither the present nor the future, nor any powers, neither height nor depth, nor anything else in all creation, will be able to separate us from the love of God that is in Christ Jesus our Lord" (Romans 8:38-39).*
"God is love" (1 John 4:8b).

PREPARATION: *You will need a Bible and a ring, preferably a wedding ring.*

The Object Lesson

(Hold the ring in your palm so children can see it.)
● What is this?
● Why do people give each other rings?
Most rings are in the shape of a circle. *(Point to the ring.)*
● Where does this circle begin, and where does it end?
When people get married, they usually give each other rings as a sign of their love. That's because love is like a circle; it has no beginning and no end. The Bible tells us that God's love is like that, too. *(Read aloud 1 John 4:8b and Romans 8:38-39.)*
● What do these passages mean?
● How does God show his love for you?
Just as people give rings as a sign of their never-ending love, God gave us something to show that his love for us will go on forever. God sent his Son, Jesus, to die for the bad things we do. Now, when we believe in Jesus, we can live forever with God. That's how much God loves each of us.

(Hold up the ring again.) A circle is a good reminder of God's love for us. I know a song that will help you remember the things we've learned today.

(Lead children in singing the following song to the tune of "Puff, the Magic Dragon.")

God's love is like a circle—
A circle big and round.
And when you see a circle,
No ending can be found.

So the love of Jesus goes on eternally.
Forever and forever,
I know that God loves me.

Prayer

God, we're glad that you are love. Thank you that your love is powerful and never-ending. You will always be with us and always love us. In Jesus' name, amen.

Who's in Control?

THEME: *Our words are very powerful.*

SCRIPTURE: *"When we put bits into the mouths of horses to make them obey us, we can turn the whole animal. Or take ships as an example. Although they are so large and are driven by strong winds, they are steered by a very small rudder...Likewise the tongue is a small part of the body"* (James 3:3-5b).

PREPARATION: *You will need a Bible, a toy horse with a bridle, and a toy ship with a rudder. (If you can't find or borrow either of the toys, bring a picture of a horse's bit and a picture of a ship's rudder.)*

The Object Lesson

(Hold up the toy horse.) Before most people ride a horse, they put something called a bit in the horse's mouth. *(Point to the bit or where the bit would go in the toy horse's mouth. The bit is simply a little metal bar that's attached to the bridle.)*

● What do you think the bit does?

● Why is the bit important?

The bit helps control the horse, making the horse go where the rider wants it to go. *(Set down the toy horse, and show children the toy ship. Point to the rudder.)*

● What is this little part?

● Why is it important?

When someone is steering a ship, he or she needs a rudder to turn the ship and help it stay on course. Without a rudder, the ship would go where the wind and waves pushed it.

● How are the rudder and the bit similar?

Rudders and bits are both small things that are used to control big things. The Bible tells us about something else that's little but powerful. *(Read aloud James 3:3-6.)*

● How is your tongue similar to the rudder and the bit?

● What important job does your tongue have?

Just like the rudder and bit, your tongue—and the words you say—can steer you in different directions. If you say unkind words, your life will go in one direction. If you say kind words, your life will take a different direction.

● Who controls the bit? The rudder? Your tongue?

If we control our tongues, it's likely that we'll still say bad things. But when we let God control the words we say, he'll help us say kind and encouraging things. It's important to make sure God's in control of all we do and say!

Prayer

Dear God, thank you for giving us the ability to speak, using only our little tongues to form words. Help us to use kind, encouraging words rather than unkind or hurtful ones. We want you to be in charge of our words and to guide us in the right way. Amen.

The "i" in Hurricane

THEME: *God wants us to control our anger.*

SCRIPTURE: *" 'In your anger do not sin': Do not let the sun go down while you are still angry" (Ephesians 4:26).*

PREPARATION: *You will need a Bible and a magazine or newspaper picture of a hurricane on land. (You should be able to find hurricane pictures at your local library.)*

The Object Lesson

(Show children the hurricane picture.)
- What do you think is happening in this picture?
- What would it be like to be in a hurricane?

(If any children have had firsthand experiences with hurricanes, allow them to share what the experiences were like.)

Although a hurricane is a big, powerful storm, it usually starts out as just a small disturbance in the ocean. Within a matter of days, that little storm can become a dangerous and destructive hurricane.

People can be a little like hurricanes. When we get angry, that little bit of anger can grow inside us until we hurt others.
- What things do you do or say when you're angry?
- How are those things like the damage that a real hurricane does?

God's Word gives us some advice about dealing with our anger. You might call it "storm control." *(Read aloud Ephesians 4:26.)*
- What does God tell us to do with our anger?
- How will those things help control our angry hurricanes?

The Bible tells us not to sin while we're angry. That means no matter how mad you feel, it's not OK to hurt yourself or someone else. The Bible also says to take care of your bad feelings before you go to bed. That way, they won't grow bigger overnight.

(Hold up the hurricane picture.) When you feel angry, think of the hurricane and practice a little of God's "storm control."

Prayer

Dear God, it can be hard for us to control our anger and keep it from growing into a storm. Help us to be forgiving and to take care of our angry feelings quickly. In Jesus' name, amen.

A Tale of Two Houses

THEME: *Jesus wants us to follow him.*

SCRIPTURE: *"Therefore everyone who hears these words of mine and puts them into practice is like a wise man who built his house on the rock" (Matthew 7:24).*

PREPARATION: *You will need a Bible, two pieces of cardboard, and plastic interlocking blocks (such as Legos). Use the blocks to build two simple houses, each on a separate piece of cardboard. When building the first house, do not interlock many of the blocks above the base layer. The house will be unstable, so you'll need to carry it carefully. When building the second house, interlock every row to make a very sturdy house.*

The Object Lesson

Jesus had lots of important things to tell people. He taught about God's love, how God wants us to live, and even how to pray. Jesus wanted people to know how important it was to listen to his words and do what he said. So he told this story.

(Read aloud Matthew 7:24-28. Then bring out the two houses and set them side by side. Point to the well-constructed house.) Let's pretend this is the first house in the story Jesus told. Let's see how this house does in a "storm." *(Have a child shake the cardboard base while other children blow on the house. After a few seconds, have the "storm" stop.)* Jesus said that a person who follows his teachings is like someone who builds a strong house.

- What do you think Jesus meant by that?
- What "storms" or hard times do you face in life?
- How does following God help you get through those "storms"?

(Point to the poorly constructed house.) Let's pretend this is the second house in the story Jesus told. *(Choose another child to shake the cardboard base while other children blow on the house. After a few seconds, stop the "storm.")* Jesus said that a person who doesn't obey his teachings is like someone who builds a house that would easily fall down.

- What do you think Jesus meant by that?
- How will your life "fall apart" if you don't follow Jesus?

Jesus wants us to build our lives on him—he's a solid foundation that will last through all the hard times that will come our way. When we follow Jesus and obey him, we're building a life that will last forever!

Prayer

Dear Jesus, thank you for teaching us the importance of building our lives on you. Thank you for helping us through life's "storms" and the hard times we face. Give us the wisdom to follow and obey you. Amen.

A Wonderful Way to Spell "Joy"

THEME: *God gives us strength through joy in him.*

SCRIPTURE: *"The joy of the Lord is your strength"* *(Nehemiah 8:10b).*

PREPARATION: *You'll need three sheets of paper and a marker. Write the letters J, O, and Y, each on a separate sheet of paper.*

The Object Lesson

In Bible times, people didn't have God's Word to read and learn from. The religious leader might have had some of the books that are in our Bibles, and he would read them to the people. One day the people all got together and asked Ezra, the religious leader, to read to them. Ezra stood up on a special wooden box and read God's laws to the people. As they listened to God's Word, the people started to cry. They were sad when they realized how far they had slipped from what God wanted them to do. Ezra and the other leaders told them not to be sad but to be happy and have a feast and give presents to those in need because this was a happy time. He said, "Do not grieve, for the joy of the Lord is your strength."

● What do you think he meant by "the joy of the Lord"?

● How can that joy make you strong?

God wants us to have joy in our lives. There's a fun way to remember how to have the joy of the Lord. All you need to know are the letters that spell joy—J, O, and Y.

(Hold up the J paper.) The J stands for Jesus—the most important thing in your life. Remember Ezra said that it was a happy time because the people could learn about God. Jesus came to show us what God is like. *(Hand the J to a child who can hold it up during the rest of the lesson.)*

(Hold up the O paper.) O stands for others. Ezra told the people to give presents to those who were in need. He wanted them to think about other people. *(Hand the O to another child, and have him or her hold it up next to the J.)*

(Hold up the Y paper.) Y represents you. That means our needs or concerns come last. *(Give the Y to another child, and have him or her hold it up next to the O. Point to the word "JOY.")* When we put Jesus first, others second, and ourselves last, we have real joy! Then we'll understand that the joy of the Lord is our strength!

Prayer

God, thank you for giving us your special joy that can help us through hard times. Help us to put Jesus first in our lives, others second, and ourselves last. We want to have real joy that comes from you. In Jesus' name, amen.

Amazing Grace

THEME: *God's grace saves us from sin.*

SCRIPTURE: *"For it is by grace you have been saved" (Ephesians 2:8a).*

PREPARATION: *You will need a Bible, a sheet of paper, a marker, and a life preserver (a simple inflatable ring will work fine). Use the marker to write the word "grace" down the left side of the paper. Using the letters as an acrostic, write the phrase "God's Riches At Christ's Expense" across the paper.*

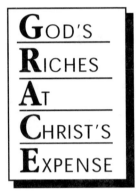

GOD'S
RICHES
AT
CHRIST'S
EXPENSE

The Object Lesson

(Hold up the life preserver.)
- What is this?
- When would I need to use it?
- What might happen if I didn't use it?
- What other things help save lives?

It's important to know how to dial 911, use a fire extinguisher, or even apply first-aid techniques. Those things can all help save people's lives. But the Bible tells us about the most important lifesaving device of all. It's something called grace.

(Read aloud Ephesians 2:8.)
- What do you think grace means?

Grace is sort of like undeserved love and forgiveness.
- What does grace save us from?

God's grace saves us from our sin. It saves us from spending eternity away from God. I know an easy way to help you understand what grace is. *(Hold up your sheet of paper. Point to the first letter of each word.)* These letters spell "grace." And there's a word written with each letter. It says "God's Riches At Christ's Expense."
- What do you think God's riches might be?

"God's riches" means lots of things—life with God in heaven, having our sins taken away, enjoying God's love, and being part of God's family. Grace means that we get all those things because Jesus Christ paid for our sins. That's what it means when we say "at Christ's expense."

- Why do you think God saved us with grace?
- How does it feel to understand grace?

Let's thank God for his wonderful grace.

Prayer

God, thank you for your amazing grace that saved all of us. Thank you for your love and Jesus' sacrifice that paid for our sins. We want to live with you forever in heaven, enjoying your riches. Amen.

One-Way Ticket

THEME: *We each have a place in heaven.*

SCRIPTURE: *"In my Father's house are many rooms; if it were not so, I would have told you. I am going there to prepare a place for you" (John 14:2).*

"They replied, 'Believe in the Lord Jesus, and you will be saved' " (Acts 16:31a).

PREPARATION: *You will need a Bible and a variety of tickets such as movie tickets, theater tickets, ball-game tickets, and plane tickets, or make tickets by cutting strips of paper and writing "Ticket" on each strip.*

The Object Lesson

(Show children the tickets, and ask what each one is for.)

● Why would I need these tickets?

● What would happen if I wanted to go to the ball game, but I didn't have a ticket?

You need a ticket to go to lots of special places or events. In fact, they won't let you in without one! Sometimes, places sell out of tickets when the stadium or building is too full. But I know of one place that will never sell out of tickets. *(Read aloud John 14:2.)*

● Where is there always enough room for you?

● What goes through your mind when you think about your place in heaven?

Even though Jesus is preparing a special place for us in heaven, we still need a sort of ticket to get in. Listen to this passage and see if you can tell what your "ticket" might be. *(Read aloud Acts 16:31a.)*

● What's your ticket to heaven?

When you believe in Jesus, it's as if you're getting a ticket to heaven. And we can trust that God will never "sell out" of tickets—there's room for everyone!

Prayer

Dear Jesus, thank you for making a way for us to live in heaven. We're glad that there's plenty of room in our heavenly Father's house. Help us to discover the importance of believing in you. Amen.

The Power Insid...

THEME: *God's power gives us strength.*

SCRIPTURE: *"The Lord gives strength t...*
29:11a).

PREPARATION: *You will need a Bible,*
and an adult volunteer. Give the remote control device to the
volunteer, and have him or her hide somewhere in the room.

The Object Lesson

(Bring out the remote control car, and set it in front of you.) Watch the amazing things my car can do! Car, go forward. *(Pause while your helper "drives" the car forward a few feet.)* Car, stop. Now go backwards. *(Continue giving commands and allowing your helper to make the car follow them.)*

- How could the car move on its own?
- Where did the power come from?

(Have the volunteer stand up and show children the remote control device.) The Bible tells us where we get our power or strength. *(Read aloud Psalm 29:11a.)*

- How does this verse remind you of the remote control car?
- Did the car work even though you couldn't see who was controlling it? Explain.

We're a lot like this car. The car needs two things in order to do all the amazing things it can do. *(Show children where the batteries go inside the car.)* The car needs batteries inside to help it do what the remote control device *(hold up the remote control device)* directs it to do. You and I need God's Holy Spirit inside us to help us do the things God wants us to do. Even though we can't see God, with God and his Holy Spirit we have the strength to face hard times and to help others face hard times.

Prayer

Dear God, thank you for giving us the strength to go through anything. Thank you for your Holy Spirit, who works inside us and gives us strength. Help us to listen and obey so that we can do what you direct us to. Amen.

aky-Clean

THEME: *Jesus washes away our sin.*

SCRIPTURE: *"Create in me a pure heart, O God" (Psalm 51:10a).*
" 'Although you wash yourself with soda and use an abundance of soap, the stain of your guilt is still before me,' declares the Sovereign Lord" (Jeremiah 2:22).

PREPARATION: *You will need a Bible and a bucket full of cleaning supplies such as laundry- and dish-detergent, a bar of soap, toothpaste, shampoo, and a scrubbing brush.*

The Object Lesson

(Read aloud Psalm 51:10a.) When this verse uses the word "heart," it means our lives.

● What would make your life impure or dirty?

I thought getting a clean life was a good idea, so I looked around the house for some cleaning supplies. (Bring out the bucket of cleaning supplies, and show them to the children.)

● What are these used for?

● Which of these do you think would help clean my life?

Let's see what the Bible says about cleaning the sin from our lives. (Read aloud Jeremiah 2:22.)

● What do you think this verse means?

We can't clean our lives with soap—God still sees our sin. Let's see if another Bible verse will help us. (Read aloud 1 John 1:7.)

● According to this verse, what purifies us from sin?

● How does Jesus' blood make us clean?

When people talk about Jesus' blood, they mean that Jesus bled and died to purify us from sin. So if we want our lives to be pure and cleansed of sin, we need to believe in Jesus. (Point to the bucket of cleaning supplies.) That sounds a lot easier than scrubbing with all these things! Let's thank God for giving us clean, pure lives.

Prayer

Dear God, thank you that we can have clean, pure hearts because of Jesus. Thank you for your love and forgiveness. We're glad that you wash away our sins and make us new. In Jesus' name, amen.

The Doubtful Dough

THEME: *God made us to fulfill his plans.*

SCRIPTURE: *"Does not the potter have the right to make out of the same lump of clay some pottery for noble purposes and some for common use?" (Romans 9:21).*

PREPARATION: *You will need a Bible and a handful of modeling dough.*

The Object Lesson

(Divide the dough into two pieces. Knead and shape the dough into different shapes.)

- What can I make with this dough?
- Who will make the final decision about what I make?

I can make just about anything with this dough. I could make something useful, like a pot, or something pretty, like beads for a necklace. But it's my decision—the dough can't tell me what I should or shouldn't make.

(Set down the dough shapes, and read aloud Romans 9:20-21.) In the Bible, there were people called potters who used clay to make pots.

- How is God like a potter?
- How are you and I like clay?

God made us exactly the way he wants us to be, just as I made the dough into the shapes that I wanted them to be. Sometimes we complain about the way God made us or the things he wants us to do. That's sort of like this dough telling me "I don't want to be a pot! I want to be a beautiful bead on a necklace!"

- Who's in charge, me or the dough?
- Who knows what's best for the dough?

God knows what's best for us, too. He's made us a certain way with certain jobs to do, because God knows everything. Although we may not always like the way God made us, we need to trust him and believe that he has a plan.

Prayer

God, thank you for creating each of us with your own hands. Help us to trust you and have faith that your plans are best for us. We know that you love us and will use us in special ways. Amen.

Big-Bang Bust

THEME: *God created the world.*

SCRIPTURE: *"In the beginning God created" (Genesis 1:1a).*

PREPARATION: *You will need a Bible and a large resealable bag filled halfway with plastic interlocking blocks.*

The Object Lesson

● What comes to your mind when you think about how the world began?

People believe many different things about how the world began. I'm going to tell you two stories about the beginning of the world, and I want you to tell me which one you think is true.

1. Millions of years ago, there was an accident out in space and something crashed. All of the proper elements accidentally came together, and the world came into being.

2. God is love, and because he is love, God created the world. He made everything with a purpose and a plan with perfect detail.

● Which idea do you think is true? Explain.

The Bible is true, and it says "In the beginning God created the heavens and the earth." I have something to illustrate just how silly the first story is.

(Bring out the bag of plastic interlocking blocks, and let children take turns shaking the bag.) We'll pretend these blocks are the elements that make up things like trees, fish, animals, and people. Some people believe that those things just fell into place accidentally. Let's see what that might be like. I'll pour the blocks on the floor. We'll see if the blocks form a house or another structure. *(Pour the blocks on the floor or into a shallow cake-pan.)*

● Wat happened to the blocks?

● Why didn't they create something?

● What would need to happen in order for us to have a block house?

● How is this similar to the way the world was created?

The world wasn't just an accident. God created each blade of grass, each tiny insect, and each gigantic whale with his own hands—just like you'd have to put each block together to build a house. You and I were created very specially, with God's purpose and plan in mind. We didn't just happen!

Prayer

Dear God, thank you for being powerful enough and loving enough to create a beautiful world. We can see your detail and creativity in everything around us. Thank you for making us in your image with such care. We love you. Amen.

A Picture of Love

THEME: *Jesus wants us to love others.*

SCRIPTURE: *" 'Love your neighbor as yourself.' " (Luke 10:27b).*

PREPARATION: *You will need a Bible, a color photograph of a person, and a photocopy of the photograph.*

The Object Lesson

Jesus often taught people that it was important to love others. In fact, his law said to "Love your neighbor as yourself." One time, someone asked Jesus, "Who is my neighbor?" This is the story Jesus used to answer that man's question.

(Read aloud Luke 10:30-37.)

- According to Jesus, who is your neighbor?
- Are your neighbors just the people you like? Explain.
- Why do you think Jesus wants us to love everyone?

(Hold up the photocopy of the photograph.) This is a picture of someone I know.

- Does this photocopy help you know what that person looks like?
- Does this picture look exactly like him (her)? Explain.

(Hold up the real photograph next to the photocopy.) Jesus is like this real picture—a crystal-clear picture that shows us what God is like. We're sort of like photocopies of Jesus. Our words and actions can show people what Jesus is like. That's why Jesus wants us to love everyone, so they can catch a glimpse of him. You may be the only view of Jesus that people see—so make it as close to the original as possible!

Prayer

Dear Jesus, help us to use our words and actions wisely to show people a picture of what you're like. Show us the way to love others, even when it's hard, so they can experience just a little of your amazing love. Amen.

Lessons for Special Occasions

Never Leave Home Without It

THEME: *Our love for others shows that we belong to God's family. (Valentine's Day)*

SCRIPTURE: *" 'By this all men will know that you are my disciples, if you love one another' " (John 13:35).*

PREPARATION: *You will need a Bible and a variety of membership cards for places such as warehouse stores, libraries, social organizations, video stores, or fitness clubs. You will also need a heart-shaped treat for each child.*

The Object Lesson

(Display the membership cards, and have children tell what each card is for.)

Each of these cards shows that I'm a member of a group.

- Why does someone need a membership card?
- What would happen if I didn't have a membership card?

Without a membership card, people wouldn't know that I was a part of that group. Members of God's family have a special sort of "card," too. Listen to this verse, and see if you can tell what it is. *(Read aloud John 13:35.)*

- How do we show that we're members of God's family?
- Why is it important to love others?
- How can you show your "membership card" to others?

Jesus said that people will know we're Christians when they see how we love others. That means every day—not just on Valentine's Day! I'm going to display my Christian membership card now by sharing something I made. *(Distribute heart-shaped cookies or candy.)*

Prayer

God, thank you for showing us your love. Help us to love others so they'll know we're part of your family. Show us new ways to love others every day. In Jesus' name, amen.

Memories

THEME: *The Lord's Supper helps us to remember God's love for us.*

SCRIPTURE: *"While they were eating, Jesus took bread, gave thanks and broke it, and gave it to his disciples saying, 'Take and eat; this is my body' " (Matthew 26:26).*

PREPARATION: *You will need a Bible and a photo album or a scrapbook filled with pictures or mementos.*

The Object Lesson

(Show children a few pages of your photo album or scrapbook. Point out significant events, friends, relatives, or memories. Close the book.)

● Why do people keep photo albums or scrapbooks?

● What other things do we do to help us remember special people or events?

Jesus told us to do something to help us remember him. *(Read aloud Matthew 26:26-29.)*

● What did Jesus want us to do?

● Why do you think Jesus wanted us to do those things?

● What did Jesus want us to remember?

Jesus wants us to remember the sacrifice he made. He doesn't ever want us to forget how much God loves us. That's why we share the Lord's Supper—to remind us of God's love and sacrifice. Let's thank God right now.

Prayer

God, thank you so much for sending Jesus to die for our sins. Help us to remember Jesus' sacrifice and your love when we share the Lord's Supper. We don't ever want to forget the price you paid so we could live with you forever. In Jesus' name, amen.

With a Grateful Heart

THEME: *God wants us to show thankfulness to him and to others. (Thanksgiving)*

SCRIPTURE: *"One of them, when he saw he was healed, came back, praising God in a loud voice. He threw himself at Jesus' feet and thanked him" (Luke 17:15-16a).*

PREPARATION: *You will need a Bible and two or three simple thank-you cards.*

The Object Lesson

(Hold up the thank-you cards, and read a few of them aloud.)
● When do you send thank-you cards?
● How do you think people feel when they get thank-you cards?
The Bible tells us about ten people who certainly had something to be thankful for. I'll read the passage, and you decide what the people could be thankful for. *(Read Luke 17:11-14.)*
● What were the lepers thankful for?
● What would you do if that happened to you?
Let's see what the ten lepers did. *(Read Luke 17:15-19.)*
● What did the lepers do?
● Why do you think only one of them came back to thank Jesus?
● Do you ever forget to thank people? Why?
Think of five things you're thankful for. *(Pause.)*
● Who can you thank for those things?
● What would be a special way to thank that person or those people?
The Bible tells us how important it is to be thankful. So today, thank that person or those people in a special way. You might give a hug, make and send a card, or sing a thank-you song. Let's offer our thanks to God right now.

Prayer

God, thank you for all the things you bless us with. We're thankful for our families, homes, country, and schools. Mostly, we're thankful that you love us. Help us to show our thankfulness to you and to others. In Jesus' name, amen.

Rockin' Roll

THEME: *On Easter, we celebrate God's power and love.*

SCRIPTURE: *"For an angel of the Lord came down from heaven and, going to the tomb, rolled back the stone and sat on it" (Matthew 28:2b).*

PREPARATION: *You will need a Bible and a large stone (approximately the size of a football).*

The Object Lesson

• What do we celebrate on Easter?
(Set the stone in front of the children.)
• How do you think this stone reminds me of Easter?
Let me read a Scripture passage about something that happened after Jesus died. See if you can tell me why a stone is important in this story. *(Read aloud Matthew 27:57-61; 28:1-7.)*
• Why was a stone important in this story?
• Why did the angel roll the stone away from the tomb?
When the angel rolled the stone away from the entrance to the tomb, it wasn't because Jesus needed help getting out. Without the big stone blocking the entrance, everybody could clearly see that Jesus had risen from the dead. God wanted everyone to see with his or her own eyes that Jesus was more powerful than death!
• Today, what things keep us from seeing God's power in our lives?
• How can you roll those "stones" away?
Sometimes problems, activities, or people keep us so busy that they block our view of what God is doing in our lives. That's why it's so important to talk to God, read your Bible, and learn more about God from your teachers and parents.
Let's make a circle and gently roll the stone around to each person while I close in prayer. When the stone comes to you, silently tell God one way that you'll be looking for him.

Prayer

Dear God, thank you for sending Jesus to die for our sins. We're so grateful that you're more powerful than death. Help us roll away the things in life that block our view of your love and power. We want to put you first in our lives. In Jesus' name, amen.

Baby Shower

THEME: *At Christmas, we celebrate God's love and Jesus' birth.*

SCRIPTURE: *"Today in the town of David a Savior has been born to you; he is Christ the Lord" (Luke 2:11).*

PREPARATION: *You will need a Bible; a bag; and a variety of baby items such as a pacifier, a bottle, a blanket, and an outfit for a newborn. Place the baby items in the bag or in a diaper bag. (These items should be easy to borrow from a church member.)*

The Object Lesson

I've brought some special items with me today. I'll show them to you, and you can see if you can tell me what I would need them for.

(Bring out the baby items, and let children tell you what each item is called and what it's used for.)

● What other things do you need for a baby?

● What would it be like for a parent who didn't have things like this for a new baby?

● Do people usually buy baby items before or after the baby is born? Explain.

It's a lot of work to prepare for a new baby. Parents need to get things like a safe crib, warm blankets, and clothes before the baby arrives. The Bible tells us about a special baby who was born in Bethlehem.

(Read aloud Luke 2:1-16.)

● What was so special about this baby, Jesus?

● Why do you think God sent his son as a tiny, helpless baby?

Even though Jesus was God's Son, he grew up just like you and I did. He probably played with friends, went to school, and had to obey his mom and dad, too! Jesus knows what it's like to be a child. He understands how you feel, no matter what you're going through.

At Christmas, we celebrate God's love and Jesus' birth. *(Point to the baby items.)* And just as a parent prepares for a baby, we can prepare our hearts to celebrate Jesus.

● What can you do to get ready to celebrate Jesus' birth?

We can thank God for Jesus, read the Bible to learn more about who Jesus was, and give our lives to loving and serving Jesus. Let's pray right now and thank God for giving his Son.

Prayer

God, thank you for loving us so much that you sent your Son as a tiny, helpless baby. Thank you that Jesus knows what it's like to be a child and to go through many of the things we go through. Help us to prepare our hearts and minds to celebrate Jesus' birth. Help us to remember the reason that he came. Amen.

Victory in Jesus

THEME: *Palm Sunday reminds us that Jesus is Lord of our lives.*

SCRIPTURE: *"They took palm branches and went out to meet him, shouting, 'Hosanna!' ' Blessed is he who comes in the name of the Lord!' " (John 12:13a).*

PREPARATION: *You will need a Bible, a pompom, and a palm branch (available at many plant nurseries). If you can't find a pompom, use a simple pennant.*

The Object Lesson

(Hold up the pompom, and shake it for a few seconds.)
- When do people use this?
- Why do they use it?

It's fun to cheer for someone we know or for a favorite team. It makes us feel happy, and it lets the person or team know that we're supporting them. In Bible times, it seems that people liked to cheer, too...except they didn't use pompoms. They used palm branches!

(Hold up the palm branch, and let children take turns waving it in the air.) Palm branches were used to celebrate a victory, sort of like the way you might wave a pompom when your favorite team wins. The Bible tells us of a certain time people waved palms.

(Read aloud John 12:12-13.)
- What were the people celebrating?
- How do we "cheer" for Jesus today?

The people in this Bible passage cheered because they wanted Jesus to be their king right then and there. They didn't understand that Jesus would be king in heaven, not on earth. Jesus also wants to be king, or Lord, of our hearts and lives. He wants us to praise him and tell everyone that "Jesus is number one!" Let's praise Jesus now.

Prayer

Dear Jesus, we want to make you Lord of our hearts and lives. We want everyone around us to know that you're number one. Thank you for loving us. Amen.

Two Precious Gifts

THEME: *On Mother's Day, we celebrate the gift our mothers gave us.*

SCRIPTURE: *"But the gift of God is eternal life in Christ Jesus our Lord" (Romans 6:23b).*

PREPARATION: *You will need a Bible.*

The Object Lesson

- Who is in your family?

Even though each of your families is different, you all have one thing in common. In fact, every person in the world has this one thing in common. Every person has a mother!

Whether you live with your mother or even know your mother, she gave you something wonderful.

- What wonderful thing do mothers give us?

Our mothers give us life! Your mom carried you around in her body for nine months—that's almost a whole year! It probably wasn't very comfortable for her. She may have been really sick, and it's likely that you kicked her in the ribs once or twice!

- Why do you think your mom went through all that discomfort?
- How does it feel to know that someone loves you that much?

Our moms went through a lot to give us the precious gift of life. God did the same thing. *(Read aloud Romans 6:23b.)*

- How did God give us life?
- What hard things did Christ go through for us?
- How does it feel to know that God loves you that much?

Every person in this room is here because of a mother's love. Every person in this room has a chance at new life because of God's love. Let's thank God for the precious gift of life—both on earth and in heaven—and those who gave us that gift.

Prayer

Dear God, thank you for our mothers, who gave us the gift of life on earth. Thank you for your gift of eternal life. We know you suffered to give it to us, but we're thankful for your love. Amen.

Daddy's Heart

THEME: *On Father's Day, we can celebrate the gift of God's love.*

SCRIPTURE: *"How great is the love the Father has lavished on us, that we should be called children of God!" (1 John 3:1a)*

PREPARATION: *You will need a Bible, a box, wrapping paper, tape, a sheet of red construction paper, and scissors. Before this lesson, cut a simple heart from the construction paper. Place the heart in the box, and wrap it.*

The Object Lesson

(Hold up the box.)
- Why do dads get presents on Father's Day?
- What kinds of presents do they often get?
- What do you think this gift might be?

This is a gift **from** a father. He wants you to have it to keep forever! And there's enough in this one box for each person here! Let me read a Bible verse to give you a clue about what's in the box and who it's from. *(Read aloud 1 John 3:1a.)*
- Who do you think this gift is from?
- What do you think it is?

Let's find out. *(Open the box, and take out the heart.)*
- What do you think this means?
- Why would God give us a gift?

When we believe in Jesus, we become a part of God's family. We're beloved children of God! This gift represents the love of God, our heavenly Father, which he poured out on us by making us his children.
- What gift can you give your heavenly Father?
- How can you honor your heavenly Father today?

God is our Father, and we are his children. On Father's Day, remember to give God your love, honor, and praise.

Prayer

Heavenly Father, thank you for your gift of love. We're glad to be your children and to call you our Father. We love you and want to praise you for all that you are and all that you do. Accept our gifts of love, time, praise, and honor. Amen.

Happy Birthday!

THEME: *We can be part of God's family.*

SCRIPTURE: *"How great is the love the Father has lavished on us, that we should be called children of God!" (1 John 3:1a)*

PREPARATION: *You will need a Bible, a cupcake, matches, a cup of water, and a birthday candle that relights itself after it is blown out. (You can find these at many party-supply stores.) Place the candle in the center of the cupcake. (Optional: You may want to supply a cupcake for each child to take home.)*

The Object Lesson

● Why do we celebrate birthdays?

Your birthday is very special because it marks the date when you were born and became a member of your family. When you believe in Jesus, you become a member of God's family. *(Read aloud 1 John 3:1a.)* Lots of people celebrate a second birthday. They celebrate the important date when they were born into God's family.

(Bring out the cupcake and the matches, and light the candle.) We'll celebrate our second birthdays with this cupcake and candle. Let's sing "Happy Birthday to You," but instead of singing "Happy Birthday, dear [name]," we'll sing "God bless you and keep you." Then we'll all blow out this candle. Ready?

(Lead children in singing "Happy Birthday to You" and blowing out the candle. Watch the candle relight itself several times.)

● How does this candle remind you of God's love?

God's love is the reason we can become part of his family. And God's love never dies—it will never "go out." Let's end our celebration by thanking God for his never-ending love.

Prayer

Dear God, we're so thankful that you allow us to be part of your family. Thank you that your love for us will never go away. We're glad that we're your children. In Jesus' name, amen.

Saint Patrick

THEME: *Saint Patrick taught people about the Trinity. (Saint Patrick's Day)*

SCRIPTURE: *" 'I and the Father are one' " (John 10:30).*
" 'And I will ask the Father, and he will give you another Counselor to be with you forever—the Spirit of truth' " (John 14:16-17a).

PREPARATION: *You will need a Bible, scissors, and green construction paper. Cut a three-leafed shamrock from the construction paper.*

The Object Lesson

In March, we celebrate Saint Patrick's Day.

● Why do we want to remember Saint Patrick?

Patrick was born in England to a wealthy Christian family. When Patrick was sixteen years old, he was captured by pirates and sold as a slave in Ireland. After six years as a slave, he escaped and went home. Patrick liked the Irish people, and he decided that he wanted to go back to Ireland to tell the people there about God. When he went back, Patrick used the three-leafed shamrock to explain that God has three parts—the Father, the Son, and the Holy Spirit.

(Read aloud John 10:30 and John 14:16-17a and then hold up the paper shamrock.)

● How do you think the shamrock reminded Patrick of those three parts?

● Would a shamrock look the same without one of its leaves? Explain.

Without one of its parts, the shamrock wouldn't be whole. God is the same way. It takes the Father, the Son, and the Holy Spirit all together to create the God we love and worship. Now when you see a three-leafed shamrock, you can remember that God has three important parts, too.

Prayer

God, we're glad that you are God the Father, God the Son, and God the Holy Spirit. Thank you for each part that loves us in a different and special way. Amen.

The Head of the Class

THEME: *We gain wisdom when we learn to respect God.*

(Note: To be used the first Sunday after school starts)

SCRIPTURE: *"The fear of the Lord is the beginning of wisdom" (Psalm 111:10a).*

PREPARATION: *You will need a Bible.*

The Object Lesson

- How do you feel when school starts in the fall?
- Why do you go to school?
- What's the best part of school?

School helps you learn lots of new things. You learn to read, write, and do math. You also learn about our country, about science, and sometimes you even learn about art and music. Those things all help you to be wise. The Bible has something to say about wisdom, too.

(Read aloud Psalm 111:10a.)

- What do you think this verse means when it talks about the fear of the Lord?

We don't have to fear God like we would a stranger or a bad person. This verse is talking about respect or awe. If we respect God and understand that he's awesome, we're on our way to becoming wise.

- What things can you do to show that you respect God?
- How can you show respect for God at school this year?

Each day, before you think about learning a spelling list or a math table, think of how you'll show that you "fear the Lord."

Prayer

God, thank you for schools and teachers who help us learn many things. Most importantly, we're thankful that we serve a wonderful and awesome God. Help us to honor and respect you with our words and our actions. We want to be wise by having a right attitude toward you. Amen.

Indexes

Scripture Index

Genesis 1:1 62
Exodus 4:1 .28
1 Samuel 16:7b 40
Nehemiah 8:10b 54
Psalm 27:14 45
Psalm 29:11a 59
Psalm 51:10a 60
Psalm 111:10a 77
Psalm 119:105 24
Psalm 127:3b 41
Proverbs 3:5-6 15
Proverbs 13:24 41
Proverbs 15:1 6
Isaiah 55:9 32
Jeremiah 2:22 60
Zechariah 13:9b 21
Matthew 5:15 29
Matthew 7:24-28 52
Matthew 11:28 22
Matthew 25:34-40 30
Matthew 26:26-29 67
Matthew 27:57-61 69
Matthew 28:1-7 69
Luke 2:1-16 70
Luke 10:27b 64
Luke 10:30-37 64
Luke 17:11-19 68
Luke 23:43 38
John 10:30 76
John 12:12-13 72
John 13:35 66

John 14:2 .58
John 14:6 .12
John 14:16-17a 76
John 15:5 .43
John 16:33b 25
Acts 3:19a 14
Acts 16:31a 58
Romans 6:23b 73
Romans 8:38-39 47
Romans 9:20-21 61
Romans 12:5-6a 20
1 Corinthians 12:4-5 19
1 Corinthians 12:27 17
Ephesians 2:8-9 . . . . .27, 56
Ephesians 4:26 51
Ephesians 4:32 . . . . .30, 31
Philippians 2:13 18
1 Timothy 2:5 10
2 Timothy 3:16 8
Hebrews 11:1 13
Hebrews 13:5b 23
James 2:1-5 40
James 2:17 36
James 3:5 .6
James 3:3-6 49
2 Peter 3:13 37
1 John 1:7 60
1 John 3:1a 74, 75
1 John 4:1-2 34
1 John 4:8b 47

Theme Index

Accepting Others 40
Anger 6, 51
The Bible 8, 24
Birthdays .75
Challenges 25
Christmas .70
Creation 62
Death 38
Discipline .41

Easter 69
Eternal Life 38
Father's Day 74
Faith 13, 36
Following Jesus 12, 43, 52, 72
Forgiveness 14, 22, 27, 60
Grace 27, 56, 60
God's Character . . .21, 23, 28, 74, 76, 77
God's Family 17, 20, 75

God's Love 47, 67
God's Plan 15, 28, 32, 61
God's Power 43, 59, 69
Heaven 37, 58
The Holy Spirit 18
Jesus 10, 12, 22, 43, 67, 69, 72
Joy 54
Kindness 30, 31
The Lord's Supper 67
Love in Action 29, 30, 31, 36, 64, 66
Mother's Day 73
Patience 45
Palm Sunday 72

Prayer 21
Saint Patrick's Day 76
School 77
Spiritual Gifts 19, 20, 61
Taming of the Tongue 49
Testing Other Teachings 34
Thanksgiving 68
Trials .23, 25
The Trinity 76
Trust 15, 22, 32, 45
Valentine's Day 66
Wisdom 77

Group Publishing, Inc.
Attention: Product Development
P.O. Box 481
Loveland, CO 80539
Fax: (970) 669-1994

Evaluation for
STRONG AND SIMPLE MESSAGES FOR CHILDREN'S MINISTRY

Please help Group Publishing, Inc., continue to provide innovative and useful resources for ministry. Please take a moment to fill out this evaluation and mail or fax it to us. Thanks!

● ● ●

1. As a whole, this book has been (circle one)

not very helpful   very helpful

1   2   3   4   5   6   7   8   9   10

2. The best things about this book:

3. Ways this book could be improved:

4. Things I will change because of this book:

5. Other books I'd like to see Group publish in the future:

6. Would you be interested in field-testing future Group products and giving us your feedback? If so, please fill in the information below:

Name _____

Street Address _____

City _____ State _____ Zip _____

Phone Number _____ Date _____